Why Did Daddy Have To Leave?
Understanding His Special Job in the Military

Story by Robert C. Snyder, Ph.D.
Illustrations by Ron Himler

Blue Marlin Publications

Why Did Daddy Have To Leave?
Understanding His Special Job in the Military

Published by Blue Marlin Publications

Text copyright © 2017 by Robert C. Snyder, Ph.D.
Illustrations copyright © 2017 by Ronald Himler

First printing 2018

Library of Congress Cataloging-in-Publication Data

Names: Snyder, Robert C., 1969- author. | Himler, Ronald, illustrator.
Title: Why did daddy have to leave? / story by Robert C. Snyder, Ph.D.,
  Military Police Captain, US Army Reserve ; illustrations by Ron Himler.
Description: Bay Shore, NY : Blue Marlin Publications, [2018] | Includes
  bibliographical references and index. | Audience: Grades K-3. | Audience:
  Ages 6-10.
Identifiers: LCCN 2018006186 | ISBN 9780988529595 (hardcover : alk. paper)
Subjects: LCSH: Children of military personnel--Juvenile literature. | United
  States. Army--Reserves--Juvenile literature. | Deployment
  (Strategy)--Psychological aspects--Juvenile literature. | Separation
  anxiety in children--Juvenile literature. | Families of military
  personnel--Juvenile literature.
Classification: LCC UB403 .S69 2018 | DDC 355.1/20973--dc23
LC record available at https://lccn.loc.gov/2018006186

ISBN 9780988529519 (softcover : alk. paper)

Job #180267

Blue Marlin Publications, Ltd.
823 Aberdeen Road, West Bay Shore, NY 11706
www.bluemarlinpubs.com

Printed and bound by Regent Publishing Services Limited in China.
Book design & layout by Jude Rich

- Robert C. Snyder, Ph.D.

To my children, Bethany and Patrick, for their sacrifices on the home front in a war they were too young to understand.

Special thanks to Josh Wolford from Haine Elementary School for his inspirational artwork recreated on page 31.

My Daddy has a special job. He is in the Army Reserve. Sometimes I miss him when he goes away for a long time. But I always know that he will come back. He says he has to do training to keep our country strong and safe.

One day, the news on TV said a war might be starting in a faraway place. I was cuddling with my Daddy when we saw the pictures of tanks and soldiers being unloaded at that faraway place. I was worried and asked my Daddy if he would have to go. He said, "For right now, I am right here." I told him that I didn't want him to have to go to war because he might get killed. Daddy said that if he did go, it would be to help our country and to help the people in the faraway country. He said that the leader of that country did very bad things and was mean to the people of his country. If my Daddy had to leave, he would be helping them have freedom like us. I was very worried. Would my Daddy have to leave?

Then one day, my Daddy got a call that said to get ready because he might have to go. I was scared! I didn't want my Daddy to leave. At night, I would hug him even tighter now. He would come in and give me extra hugs and kisses and tell me how much he loved me.

My Daddy and Mommy spent a lot of time getting all kinds of papers ready. Daddy said he felt bad that it took time away from playing with me, but it was stuff that would help Mommy take care of things just in case he would have to go. I tried to play and do things like always, but sometimes I got scared. How long would my Daddy be gone? Where would he be? Would he still love me? Why did Daddy have to leave?

I watched Daddy packing his army stuff on top of his bed. He was packing T-shirts, Army uniforms, and his helmet all in a green sack. I didn't want to bother him too much, but it made me feel better to keep going to him and giving him big hugs while he worked at packing up. I knew he liked my hugs because he squeezed me tighter and longer each time. I was still confused. If he loved me this much, why did Daddy have to leave?

A couple of weeks later my Daddy got another call. This one said he had to go to an Army base in Maryland. I was glad he was not going to the faraway place with the war. Daddy said he had to go to Maryland to train. It was too far away for him to come home, but we visited on some weekends. Daddy couldn't go far from Maryland in case he got called to go on an airplane to go help with the war. But my Daddy always told me that he loved me no matter what, even if he was far away. I still wondered why my Daddy had to leave.

When we visited Daddy, I ran and jumped in his arms. He held me really tight even though his arms were sore. He had to get a lot of shots, in case he went to that faraway place. The shots would help him so he wouldn't get sick from diseases there.

We got to stay in a hotel room. It was fun because our whole family got to be together. It was like a sleepover party. When the weekend was over, we said goodbye to Daddy. I asked him if we would see him next weekend. He said he didn't know, but no matter what, he loved me. I was sad on the trip home and cried! Why did Daddy have to leave?

A couple of weeks later, Daddy surprised us at home. He came home on leave. We played checkers together, and he took me to ice skating practice. And we hugged a lot.

The news showed terrible things in the faraway country. There were explosions, bombs, and tanks. I was glad my Daddy was still safe at home. Soon, Daddy had to say goodbye and go back to his training place in Maryland. He said it might be the last time he would get to come home for a while because they were done with their training and were waiting to see where they would have to go. I asked him why he had to leave. He said sometimes people had to do things that they didn't want to do, but they had to do these things in order to make the world a better place.

I didn't see my Daddy again for a long time because he flew to that faraway country. He called sometimes when he had a phone. Daddy said he missed and loved me more than anything in the world. He also said he was glad that he was helping people there to rebuild their country. He said the little boys and girls didn't even have any food. Daddy said that the kids there always reminded him of me, especially when he would hand them a piece of candy, and they would smile. He said many of the kids did not even have shoes or clothes to wear. I was glad to know my Daddy was helping those kids.

I missed my Daddy a lot, though, especially when he had to miss my birthday party and my skating solo. I really missed him when we had to eat Thanksgiving dinner without him and when we had to open Christmas presents without him there to help me put my toys together. I liked it when I got letters in the mail from him. He always wrote that he was sad to be away and that he missed me and Mommy very much.

He also said he didn't have a lot of things like hot food, showers, and TV. He had to live in a hot desert in a tent.

I was proud of my Daddy for helping the people of this country. I still worried about him all the time. But now I started to feel like I knew why my Daddy had to leave.

Finally one day, after a very long time, we found out that Daddy would be coming home! Mommy told me that Daddy had finished his job of helping the people. He worked hard to help the kids, but I found out he did more than that. He also helped open up the jails to hold the bad people and helped train new police men and women so that this country could protect its people and make sure they were safe like us. Now I felt a little more like I knew why Daddy had to leave.

Mommy drove me to the airport. I carried a poster that I made that had an American flag I colored, and I wrote the words, "Welcome home Daddy! I love you!"

When Daddy walked down the steps of the airplane, my heart was beating really fast. I was so excited, but what would Daddy be like? Would he look the same as before? He looked different with his short hair and in his light brown desert uniform. When he saw us, he hugged me really tight and said he loved and missed me so much. It made me cry. I knew right then that he would never change when it came to being my Daddy.

On the way home and for a long time after that, my Daddy played with me, and pretty soon it seemed like he had never even gone away. But he did go away, and I am very proud of why my Daddy had to leave!

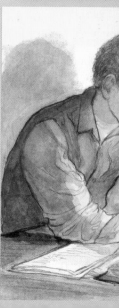